Uppercase Letters

A B C D E F G

H I J K L M N

O P Q R S T

U V W X Y Z

Lowercase Letters

a b c d e f g h i j k l m n

o p q r s t u v w x y z

CD-104349

1

Trace and write the letters.

CD-104349

Trace and write the letters.

a   a

a   a

a   a

a

Trace and write the letters.

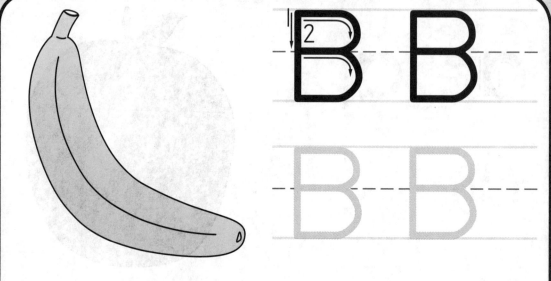

B B B B

B B

B

Trace and write the letters.

Trace and write the letters.

C C

C C

C C

C

Trace and write the letters.

C   C

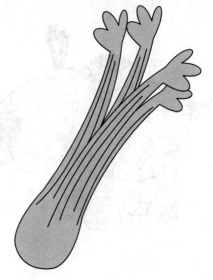

C   C

C   C

C

Trace and write the letters.

D D D

D D

D D

D

Trace and write the letters.

d d

d d

d d

d

Trace and write the letters.

CD-104349   © Carson-Dellosa

Trace and write the letters.

e   e

e   e

e   e

e

CD-104349

Trace and write the letters.

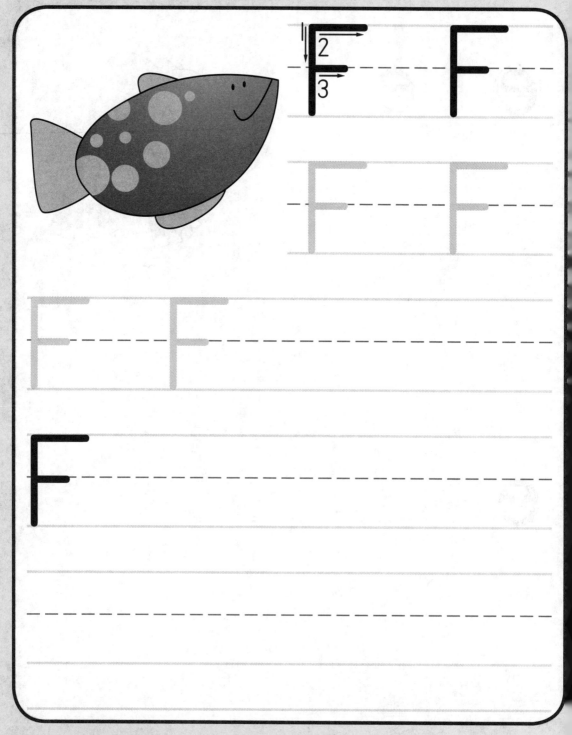

CD-104349 © Carson-Dellosa

Trace and write the letters.

Trace and write the letters.

G G

G G

G G

G

CD-104349

Trace and write the letters.

g   g

g   g

g   g

g

Trace and write the letters.

CD-104349 © Carson-Dellosa

Trace and write the letters.

Trace and write the letters.

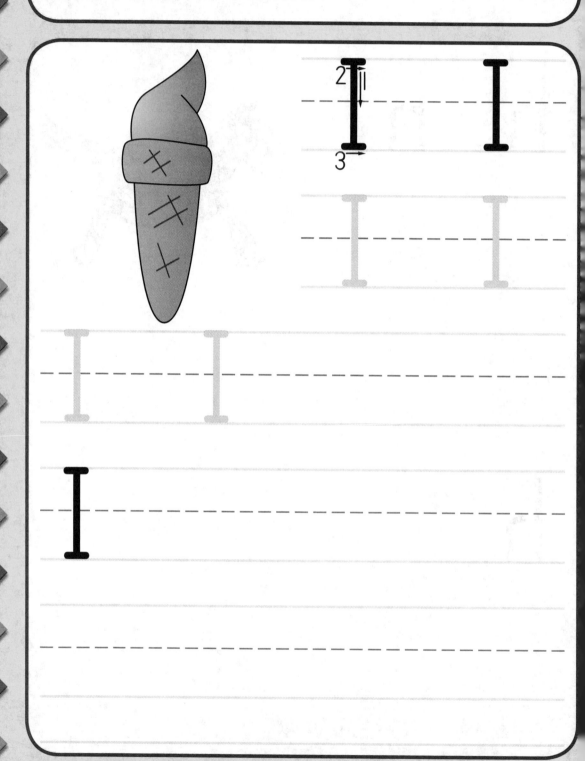

CD-104349 © Carson-Dellosa

Trace and write the letters.

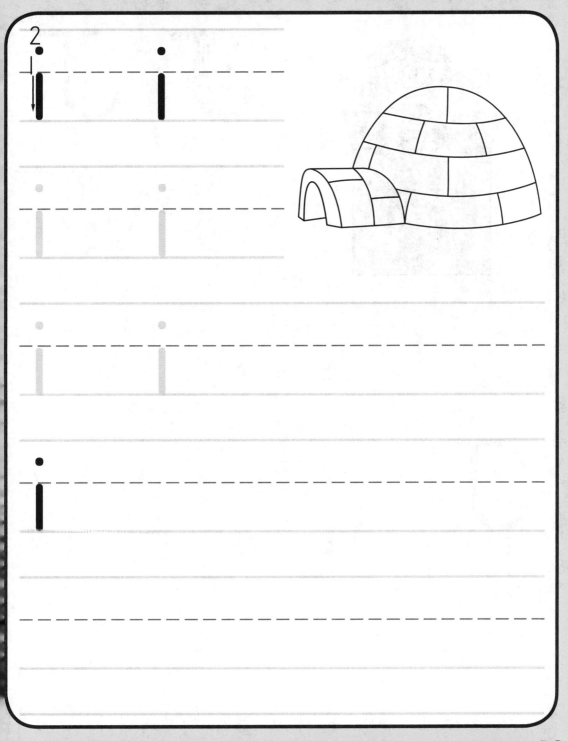

Trace and write the letters.

CD-104349

Trace and write the letters.

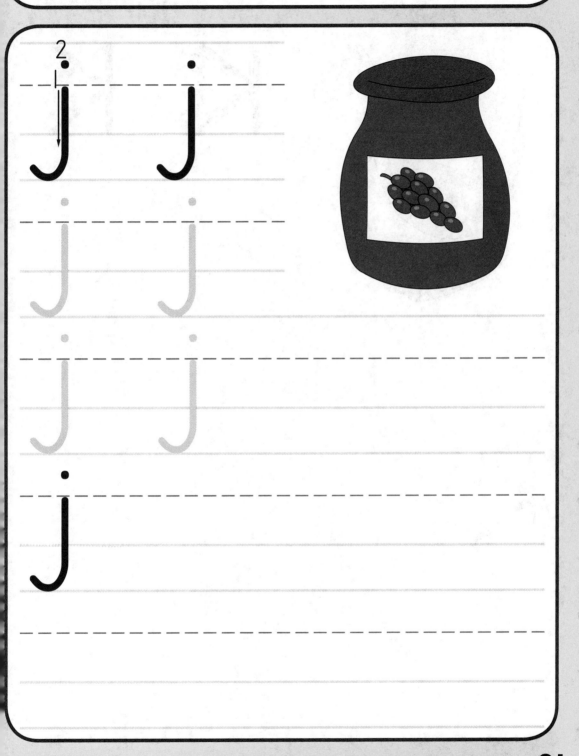

Trace and write the letters.

CD-104349 © Carson-Dellosa

Trace and write the letters.

Trace and write the letters.

CD-104349

Trace and write the letters.

Trace and write the letters.

CD-104349

Trace and write the letters.

m m

m m

m m

m

Trace and write the letters.

CD-104349

Trace and write the letters.

n   n

n   n

n   n

n

Trace and write the letters.

CD-104349 © Carson-Dellosa

Trace and write the letters.

O   O

O   O

O   O

O

CD-104349

31

Trace and write the letters.

 CD-104349

Trace and write the letters.

p   p

p   p

p   p

p

CD-104349 **33**

Trace and write the letters.

 CD-104349

Trace and write the letters.

Trace and write the letters.

R R

R R

R R

R

 CD-104349

Trace and write the letters.

r r

r r

r r

r

CD-104349 **37**

Trace and write the letters.

S S S

S S

S S

S

Trace and write the letters.

S S   S

S S   S

S S   S

S

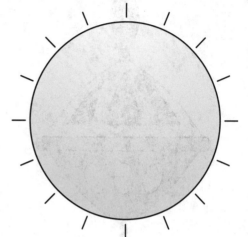

Trace and write the letters.

CD-104349

Trace and write the letters.

Trace and write the letters.

CD-104349

Trace and write the letters.

u   u

u   u

u   u

u

Trace and write the letters.

CD-104349 © Carson-Dellosa

Trace and write the letters.

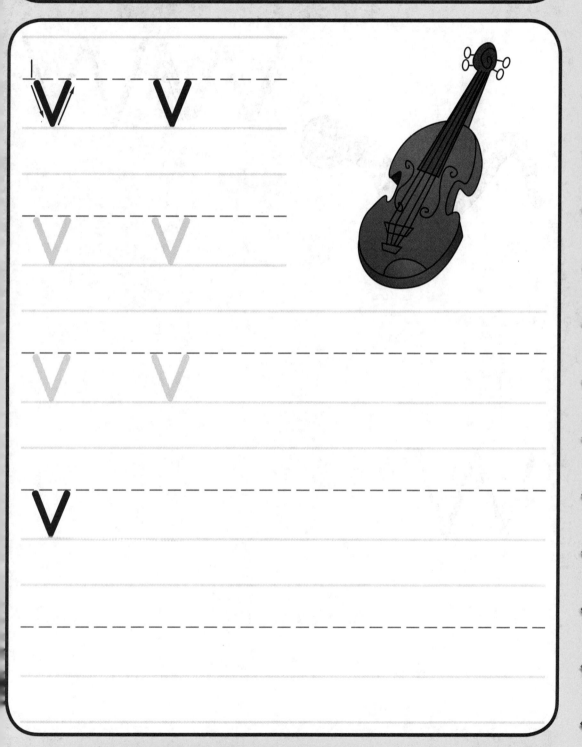

Trace and write the letters.

 CD-104349

Trace and write the letters.

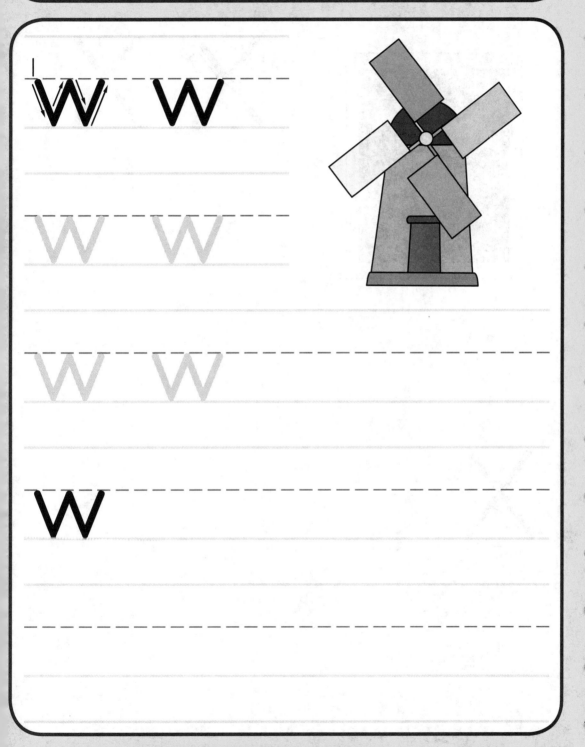

W W

W W

W W

W

Trace and write the letters.

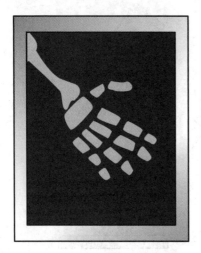

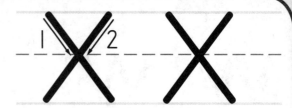

CD-104349 © Carson-Dellosa

Trace and write the letters.

Trace and write the letters.

CD-104349 © Carson-Dellosa

Trace and write the letters.

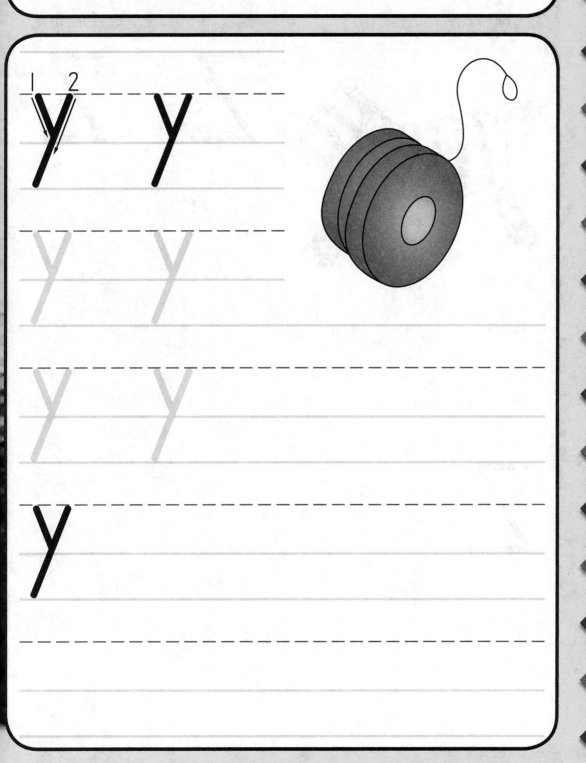

Trace and write the letters.

Z Z

Z Z

Z Z

Z

Trace and write the letters.

Z Z

Z Z

Z Z

Z

CD-104349 **53**

Draw lines to connect the matching uppercase and lowercase letters.

M   u

H   v

W   n

V   m

N   h

U   w

CD-104349

Draw lines to connect the matching uppercase and lowercase letters.

B

P

Q

G

D

R

q

g

p

r

b

d

Draw lines to connect the matching uppercase and lowercase letters.

Y	z
A	c
O	a
Z	s
C	e
E	y
S	o

CD-104349

Draw lines to connect the matching uppercase and lowercase letters.

J

L

X

F

K

I

T

x

j

i

k

t

f

l

Write the missing uppercase and lowercase letters.

A

b

c

D

E

f

G

H

CD-104349

© Carson-Dellosa

Write the missing uppercase and lowercase letters.

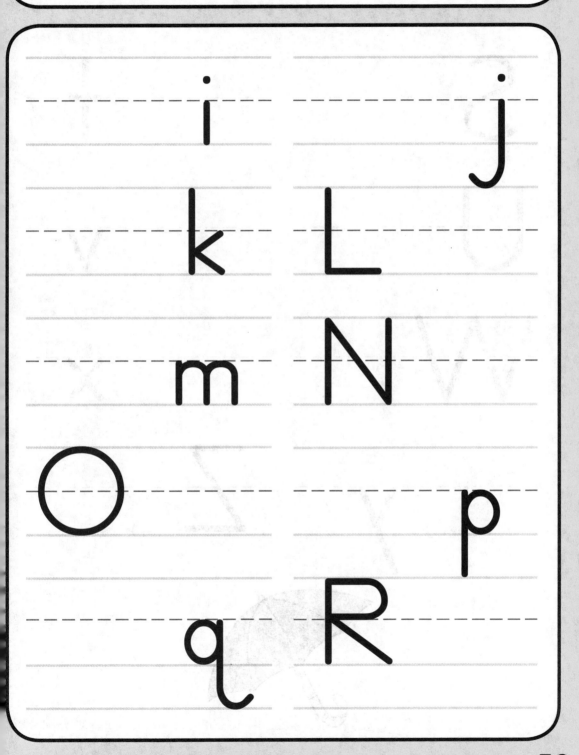

i   j

k   L

m   N

O   p

q   R

CD-104349   **59**

Write the missing uppercase and lowercase letters.

S   t

U   v

W   x

     y   Z

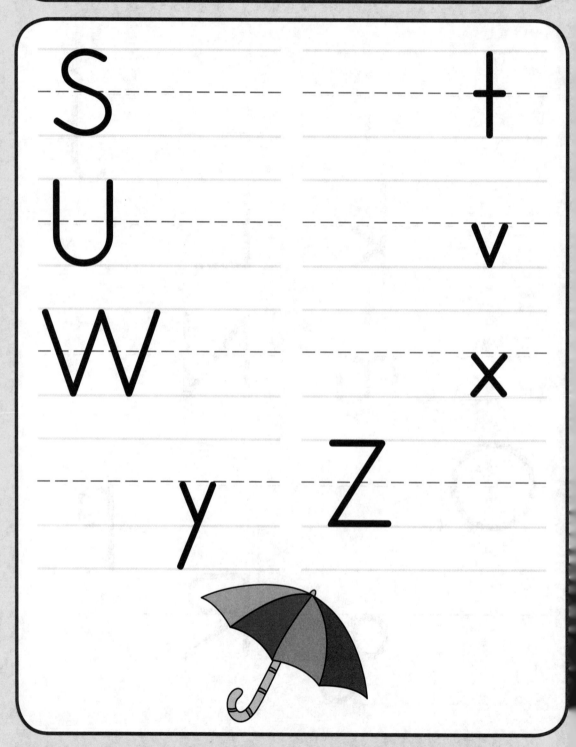

CD-104349

Trace and write the numbers.

0 0

1 1

2 2

3 3

4 4

Trace and write the numbers.

5 5

6 6

7 7

8 8

9 9

CD-104349   © Carson-Dellosa

Count the objects in each set. Write the correct number.

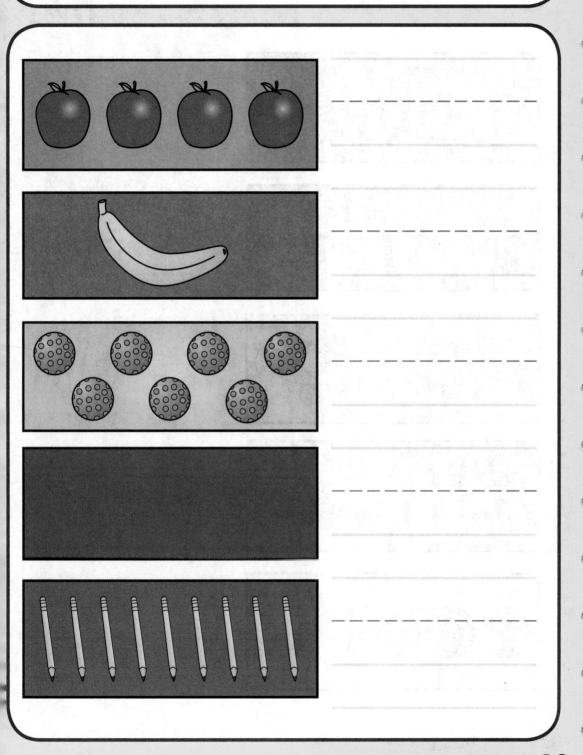

Count the objects in each set. Write the correct number.

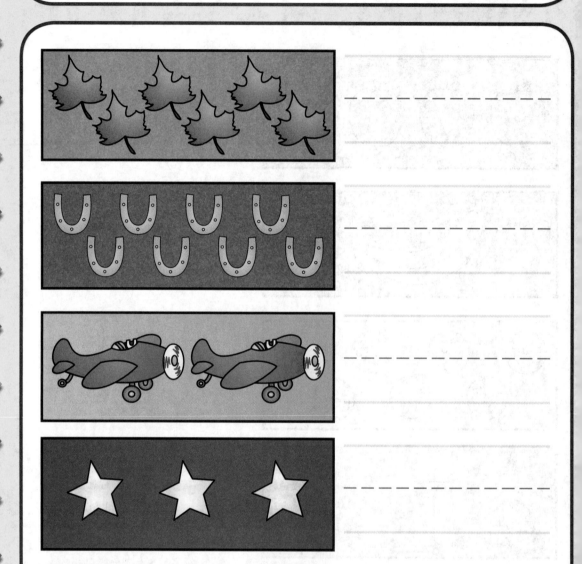
